PANDAS

Panda Magic for Kids

For R. J. and Max the dog
        — Kathy Feeney

For a free color catalog describing Gareth Stevens Publishing's list of high-quality books and multimedia programs, call 1-800-542-2595 (USA) or 1-800-461-9120 (Canada). Gareth Stevens Publishing's Fax: 414-225-0377.

Library of Congress Cataloging-in-Publication Data

Feeney, Kathy, 1954-
        Panda magic for kids / by Kathy Feeney; photography by
Tom and Pat Leeson; illustrated by John F. McGee.
                p. cm. (Animal magic for kids)
        "Based on the book, Pandas for kids . . . by Kathy Feeney" —
T.p. verso.
        Includes bibliographical references and index.
        Summary: Ten-year-old May learns about the appearance and
behavior of the giant panda, a symbol for China and a member of
an endangered species.
        ISBN 0-8368-2636-1 (lib. bdg.)
        1. Giant panda—Juvenile literature. [1. Giant panda. 2. Pandas.]
I. Leeson, Tom, ill. II. Leeson, Pat, ill. III. McGee, John F., ill.
IV. Title. V. Series.
QL737.C214F427   2000
599.789—dc21   99-053263

First published in this edition in
North America in 2000 by
Gareth Stevens Publishing
1555 North RiverCenter Drive, Suite 201
Milwaukee, WI 53212 USA

Based on the book, *Pandas for Kids*, text © 1997 by Kathy Feeney, with illustrations by John F. McGee. First published in the United States in 1997 by NorthWord Press, Inc., (Creative Publishing International), 5900 Green Oak Drive, Minnetonka, MN 55343. End matter © 2000 by Gareth Stevens, Inc.

Photographs © 1997 by Tom and Pat Leeson. Additional photography © Pan Wenshi/ National Geographic Image Collection, 36-37; Lu Zhi/National Geographic Image Collection, 34-35.

Printed in the United States of America

1 2 3 4 5 6 7 8 9 04 03 02 01 00

by Kathy Feeney

PANDAS

Panda Magic for Kids

All of the photographs in this book are of giant pandas unless noted.

Gareth Stevens Publishing
MILWAUKEE

One summer I saw a panda. A real one, not a stuffed animal in a toy store. Real pandas are from China. That is where Grandfather grew up.

My name is May, and I'm 10 years old, going on 11.

I have always loved pandas. When I was little, Grandfather gave me a toy panda for my birthday. And then one summer he took me to a zoo to see two visiting pandas.

They were awesome! I saw one somersault across the grass. The other one went splashing through a waterfall. Someday I hope to travel to China with Grandfather and see a panda in the wild.

The panda is a symbol for China, like the bald eagle is for the United States. China lends pandas to a few zoos around the world. They share pandas so people can learn about them by seeing them.

Not everyone can see one, even if you live in China. When Grandfather was a boy, many pandas wandered the dense bamboo forests near his village. Now they are very rare.

Scientists think there could be fewer than 1,000 pandas left in the wild.

The giant panda is an endangered species.

Pandas are an endangered species, which means that they might one day become extinct. But it also means that there is still time to save them.

Grandfather's brother, Uncle Lee, is a biologist. He works at a research station in a place called a panda reserve.

The Chinese government creates reserves to protect the panda. Like an oasis in the desert, a research station is a sanctuary within the panda's natural habitat.

Scientists also take pandas to research stations if they become sick or injured.

Resting on a log, this panda is at home in the remote misty mountains of China.

When Grandfather
came to live with
my parents and me,
he told us many
panda stories. He also
read his letters from
Uncle Lee to us.

Grandfather said
I would find out even
more about pandas
if I wrote to Uncle Lee
myself. I thought I knew
everything about pandas.

Then Uncle Lee
and I became pen pals.
Every time I get a
letter from Uncle Lee,
I learn something new.

*The shy and gentle panda likes
to live alone.*

Some ancestors of the panda
lived about 3 million years
ago in Asia, in places
we now call Burma,
Laos, Vietnam
and China.
Today pandas
are found only
in the mountains
of China.

Their real name
is giant panda.
Their Chinese name
is daxiong mao (that's
pronounced dah-
shwing MA-hoo).

CHINA

VIETNAM

LAOS

BURMA

VIETNAM

Most people just call them pandas. Even though "giant" is part of their name, pandas aren't really that big. It would take about 50 pandas to weigh as much as one elephant.

Pandas do have a giant white face with black patches around dark brown eyes. They have a black nose, white whiskers, and a pink tongue. Their round, black ears wiggle when they chew bamboo.

This panda munches a stalk of bamboo. Bamboo is 99 percent of the panda's diet.

Pandas are plump with short strong legs and stubby white tails. They walk "pigeon-toed," with their front feet turned inward. Lumbering through the misty mountains with their heads held low, pandas appear slow and clumsy.

"However, they are quite coordinated," wrote Uncle Lee. "Pandas are great climbers with amazing balance. They trot like horses when they're startled. And they even swim through mountain streams."

Some scientists believe the panda's black-and-white coat helps it blend into the shadowy bamboo forests.

15

Pandas climb trees when they need a safe place to hide or sleep, but they spend most of their time walking the forest floor.

They have natural snowshoes for feet. The pads of their paws are covered with fur, making it easy for them to walk on snowy slopes and icy rocks in winter.

Grandfather believes pandas are so popular because they're so peaceful. Some people say they're popular because they are so rare. I think it's because they look so soft and gentle.

The panda's thick and stiff fur is like a waterproof coat, protecting it from rain and snow.

"They may seem soft," said Grandfather. "But panda fur is really rough."

Touching a panda would feel like petting a dog with a bristly coat.

"Unlike dogs and children, pandas get clean by rolling in dirt!" said Grandfather. "They then comb the dirt out of their coats with their claws and wash up by licking their fur."

Uncle Lee sent me a drawing of a panda. It shows that the skin underneath the panda's coat is two different colors. Under the white fur is pink skin. Beneath the black fur is dark skin.

Some biologists say their color combination helps pandas blend into the shadowy forests to avoid danger.

Pandas have excellent senses of smell and hearing. Scientists have trouble tracking them because pandas hide when they smell and hear humans coming. Yet pandas have poor eyesight.

"Sometimes they walk right past their food without seeing it," Uncle Lee wrote in one of his letters.

Pandas are shy and gentle. But they have razor sharp claws for grasping bamboo. That's their favorite food. Bamboo is a hollow grass that can grow as thick as a broomstick and as tall as a telephone pole.

A panda eats about 25,000 pounds of bamboo in one year. That's about the weight of 10 big cars!

Pandas pause for a meal wherever they find bamboo.

Pages 22-23: Pandas sometimes eat while lying on their backs, sides, or bellies.

Scientists say bamboo is 99 percent of the panda's diet. Pandas need to eat a lot of bamboo because it doesn't give them much nourishment. They also like to snack on fruit, roots, wildflowers, and even birds, fish and eggs.

When Grandfather and Uncle Lee were boys, they saw a panda sneaking honey from a beehive!

Pandas nibble nearly all day and into the night. They spend up to 14 hours a day just eating. Imagine if people woke up in the morning and did nothing but eat until they went to bed.

It's no wonder pandas grow up to 5 feet long and weigh between 200 and 350 pounds.

When they're not munching their way through the bamboo forest, pandas sleep. They nap 2 to 4 hours at a time, sprawled either on their sides, backs or bellies. Sometimes pandas snore while they snooze, just like Grandfather in his favorite chair!

Some people call them panda bears. "But a panda may not be a bear at all," wrote Uncle Lee. "Nobody really knows what they are. Some scientists think pandas are related to bears because they look so much alike. Both have round heads, fat bodies and thick fur."

Pandas sometimes snack on wildflowers.

But there are also some differences between the two. For instance, pandas don't hibernate like some bears do. And their teeth are different. Like most bears, pandas have 42 teeth. But a panda's wide back teeth are powerful and very large—perfect for crushing and grinding bamboo.

There is another panda in China, called the lesser or red panda. Most scientists agree that the red panda is probably related to the raccoon.

It is about the size of a large cat. The red panda has a fox-like face with pointed ears, soft reddish brown fur and a long bushy tail.

Red pandas also love bamboo, but eat only the leaves and stems. They cannot eat the woody stalks.

The red panda shares part of the giant panda's name, but it is a closer cousin to raccoons than to bears.

Giant pandas have five fingers on each of their front paws. They also have a special "thumb." They use their thumbs to grab and hold bamboo. They usually eat sitting up, with their legs stretched out straight in front of them. Grasping bamboo stalks with their front paws, they use their fingers and thumbs to peel away the tough outer layers before eating the tender centers.

Pandas are solitary, which means they like to be by themselves. Pandas live with each other only when they are ready to mate or when a mother is raising her cub.

Pandas roam the forests searching for bamboo, so they may sleep in a different place each night.

But pandas are
never really alone.
They create silent
messages for each
other by clawing
the trunks of trees.
The scratched-off bark says:
"I'm a panda, and I've been
here."

Giant pandas are shy and
normally quiet. When they
do talk, pandas bark, bleat,
chirp, growl, honk, roar,
snort, squeal or yip.

Uncle Lee has learned
the meaning of each sound.

"Pandas in danger bark like dogs," he wrote. "When they are afraid, they squeal like pigs. During courtship, the males roar like bears."

A panda's daily search for bamboo keeps it wandering through the forest, so it doesn't really have a permanent home.

Pandas have strong jaws and sharp teeth—just what they need to tear apart tough plants.

Males and females get together in the spring to mate. After mating, the male and female go their separate ways. For the next five months, the mother prepares for the birth of her cub. She makes a bed of bamboo twigs and grasses in a cave, a hollow tree or among some rocks.

"Keeping her cub hidden is most important," said Grandfather, "because leopards and wild dogs will prey on baby pandas."

In autumn, mother pandas give birth to one or two babies. A newborn panda is so small it could fit in the palm of a person's hand. Its cry sounds like a human baby. It doesn't even look like a panda. It is pink with fine white fur. By the time the cub is a month old, it has its black-and-white markings.

Black-and-white markings appear at about one month.

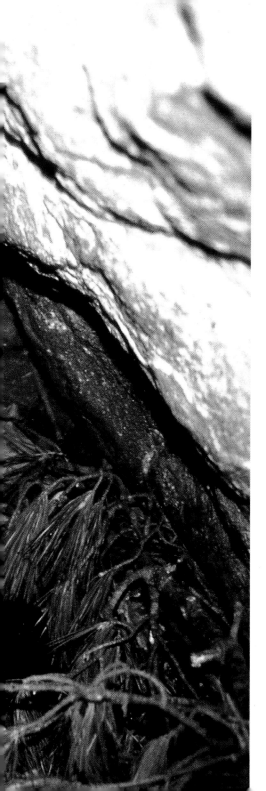

Baby pandas nurse for up to 14 hours a day. When the mother needs to find her own food, she leaves the den, holding the cub close to her chest with one paw while walking on just three legs. As the baby grows, she carries it with her mouth, like a cat.

A cub is born with its eyes closed. It sees for the first time at two months old. By five months, it has stopped nursing and begins to eat soft stalks of bamboo. At one year, a cub weighs around 70 pounds.

When not roaming in search of food, a mother panda and her cub may hide in a cave.

Before its second birthday, a panda is prepared to leave its mother and begin living on its own. Around 4 years old, pandas are mature enough to start families of their own. Scientists say pandas in the wild can live to be about 25 years old.

No matter what age they are, pandas always enjoy playing.

Uncle Lee saw one sledding through the snow. The panda slid down a hill on its belly, climbed back up, and slid all the way back down again!

People outside of China didn't even know about the giant panda until modern times. Americans first saw a panda in 1936.

People are not allowed to capture giant pandas in the wild, and killing one would be a serious crime. The Chinese government protects them. Pandas are thought of as their national treasure.

One threat to the panda is the destruction of bamboo forests. As people cut down trees for logs and build villages farther into the forests, pandas lose their habitat and must travel higher and higher into the mountains for bamboo.

Pandas are excellent climbers, even though they spend most of their time on the ground.

Pages 42-43: From nose to tail, pandas are about 5 feet long.

Uncle Lee and other scientists are working to save the panda.

When they find a panda, the researchers give it a shot so it will fall asleep. The scientists then measure and weigh the panda and check its teeth to find out its age. Before it is released, they attach a radio collar around its neck. By listening to a special machine that receives beeps from the collar, they can follow the panda through the forest and learn more about how it lives.

Just as I was daydreaming about how much fun it would be to study a panda in the wild, Grandfather called to me.

"Special delivery for May!"

It was a package from China. It was larger than Uncle Lee's other letters and was labeled **PHOTOGRAPH: DO NOT BEND!**

The panda is one of the most popular animals in the world.

Grandfather watched while I opened it. Inside was a big picture of Uncle Lee kneeling beside a young giant panda. The panda was wearing a radio collar.

"We are ready to release this panda back into the wild," Uncle Lee wrote. "Perhaps you can help us track her when you come to visit me in China one day. We call this panda something very special."

Her name is May!

GLOSSARY

Biologist: A scientist who studies plants and animals (pages 9, 19).

Endangered: At risk of dying out (pages 5, 6, 9).

Extinct: No longer living (page 9).

Habitat: A place in nature where an animal or plant lives (pages 9, 40).

Hibernate: To spend the winter asleep or in a resting state (page 29).

Nourishment: Food substances that provide health (page 24).

Nurse (v): To nourish a baby with milk from the mother (page 37).

Oasis: An area of a desert where plants grow and water is available (page 9).

Sanctuary: A safe, peaceful place (page 9).

MORE BOOKS TO READ

Giant Pandas by Sandra Lee (Child's World)

Giant Pandas by Ovid K. Wong (Children's Press)

Giant Pandas: Gifts from China by Allan Fowler (Children's Press)

Mammals. Wonderful World of Animals (series) by Beatrice MacLeod (Gareth Stevens)

The Modern Ark: Saving Endangered Species by Daniel Cohen (Putnam)

Pandas by Heather Angel (Voyageur)

VIDEOS

Panda-monium (Library Video)

Pandas with Debra Winger (Library Video)

Pandas in Person (Quality Video/Multimedia, Inc.)

WEB SITES

www.uccs.edu/~bmammend/China.htm

www.wwf.org/species/

Some web sites stay current longer than others. For further web sites, use your search engines to locate the following topics: *endangered species, giant pandas, lesser pandas, pandas, red pandas,* and *wildlife of China.*